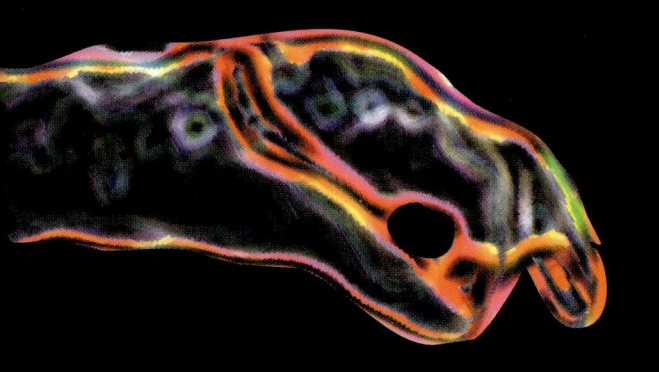

VIRTUAL REALITY

EXPERIENCING ILLUSION

CHRISTOPHER W. BAKER

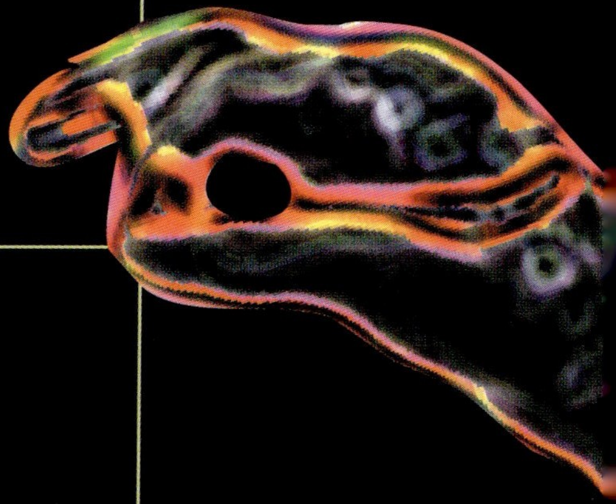

NEW CENTURY TECHNOLOGY

THE MILLBROOK PRESS
BROOKFIELD, CONNECTICUT

A note about the art in this book: Virtual reality imagery is often created for video projection and head-mounted displays, and so is generated at the lower resolutions appropriate for those media. These images, therefore, can lose clarity when printed.

Photographs courtesy of: Imprint Interactive and the University of Washington HIT Lab: p. 4; Imprint Interactive and Computer Adventures: p. 6; University of Utah, Department of Computer Science: p. 7; Airforce Research Lab: pp. 8, 9; Virtual Research: p. 10 (left); Fakespace, Inc. and Autometric, Inc.: p. 10 (right); VRAC, Iowa State University: pp. 11, 25, 33, 42, 43; NAMCO Ltd. (all rights reserved): p. 17; Fakespace, Inc. and Infobyte: p. 18; University of North Carolina, Department of Computer Science: pp. 19, 27, 31 (bottom), 36, 37 (top left); Naval Postgraduate School: pp. 21, 22; Fakespace, Inc.: p. 23; University of Tsukuba, Institute of Engineering Mechanics: p. 24; Trimension Systems: p. 28; SenseAble Technologies: p. 31 (top); University of Colorado, Center for Human Simulation: pp. 34, 35; Massachusetts Institute of Technology, Department of Computer Science and Brigham and Women's Hospital: p. 37 (top right and bottom); Naval Ocean Systems Center: pp. 38, 39, 40.

Library of Congress Cataloging-in-Publication Data
Baker, Christopher W.
Virtual reality : experiencing illusion / Christopher W. Baker
p. cm. — (New century technology)
Includes bibliographical references and index.
ISBN 0-7613-1350-8 (lib. bdg.)
1. Human-computer interaction. 2. Virtual reality. I. Title. II. Series.
QA76.9.H85B35 2000 006—dc21 99-34200 CIP

Published by The Millbrook Press, Inc.
2 Old New Milford Road
Brookfield, Connecticut 06804
www.millbrookpress.com

Copyright © 2000 by Christopher W. Baker
All rights reserved
Printed in Hong Kong
5   4   3   2

VIRTUAL REALITY

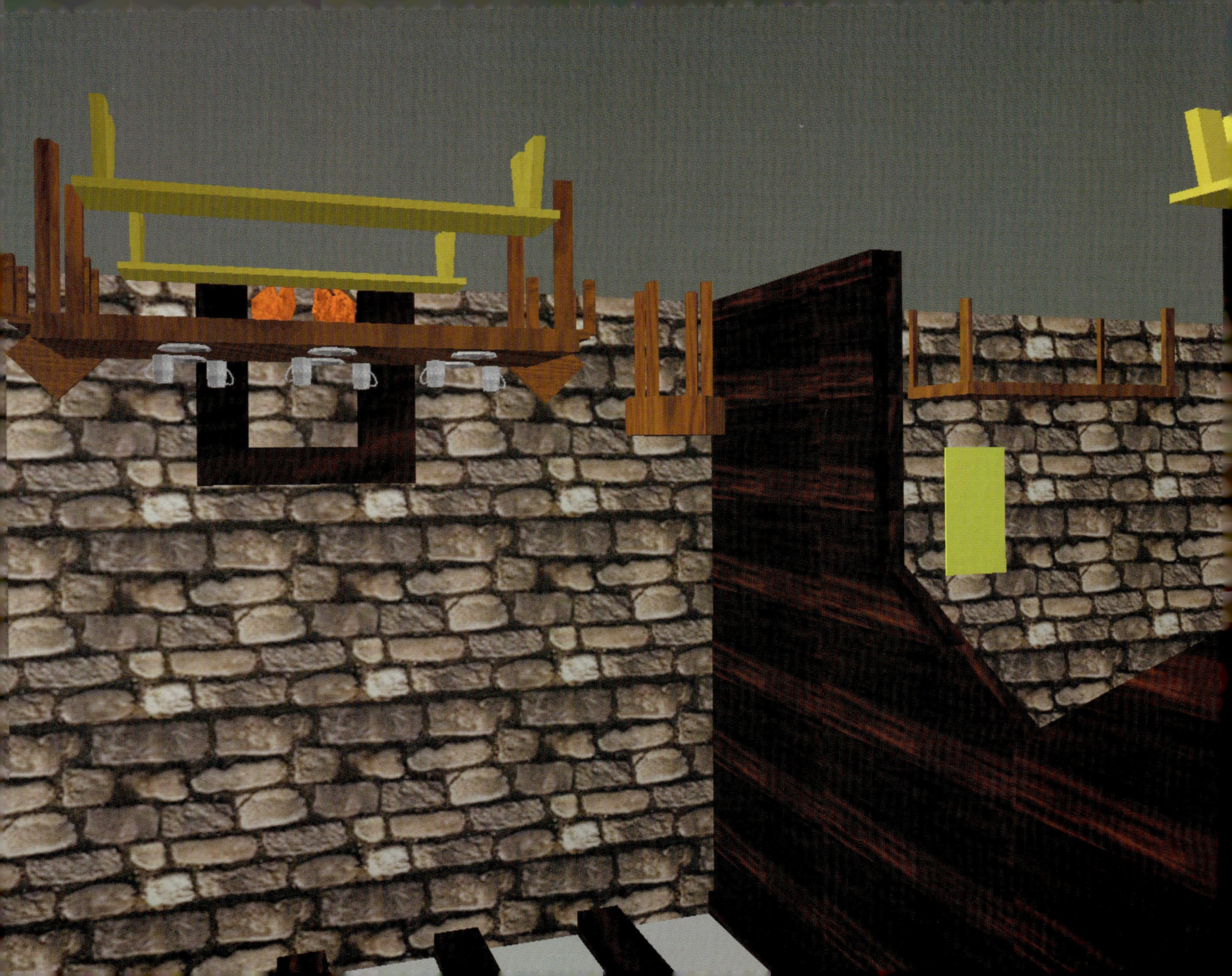

A VIRTUAL ADVENTURE

A whispered hiss from the right brings you to a halt. You turn slowly, nervously. Your friend, hiding in a doorway across the castle's stone corridor, silently points ahead. There's something beyond the next turn. You can see its shadow flickering in the torchlight.

Slowly you edge forward, weapon ready. Behind you the rush of water from the underground river almost masks the sound of claws scratching on stone. But there is no mistaking the growing stench of what is coming.

You wave your partner forward. She dodges out from the doorway into the dark of another doorway, aiming her laser toward the bend ahead. Then, in a sudden rush, the beast charges, its monstrous thudding footfalls vibrating into the soles of your feet. As it comes into sight you suddenly hear a distant call.

". . . Dinner! . . . Time for dinner!"

. . . Dinner? But the next level . . .!

"... Dinnertime!" The voice is closer, almost right behind you. In exasperation you click PAUSE on your weapon's gun sight menu, freezing the monster in mid-charge.

Looking to your partner, you shake your head. "Gotta go ... See you tomorrow." Her shoulders slump in disappointment as you pull the Surround Helmet from your head and the TouchGloves and ImpactSoles from your hands and feet. The game is over, at least for now. The Internet connection with your friend, and the world you shared, dissolves, and you turn to face your mother at your bedroom door.

Is this a day in some future life? If so, it is not so very far off. In fact, almost everything in the above story is possible with today's technology. Sight, touch, hearing, and even smell are being brought under the control of computers to create compelling and believable worlds for entertainment, science, and industry. These worlds may not be reality, but they are virtual reality.

At the Computer Adventures computer camp in Washington State kids create and explore their own virtual games and environments.

THE START OF AN ILLUSION

In many ways virtual reality (VR) seems like magic. Wave the VR wand, and suddenly you are transported into a new world where almost anything you can imagine becomes possible. The truth is, however, that these new worlds do not create themselves with a single wish. Virtual reality is the result of over thirty-five years of serious scientific effort by thousands of people around the planet.

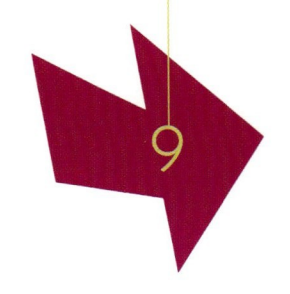

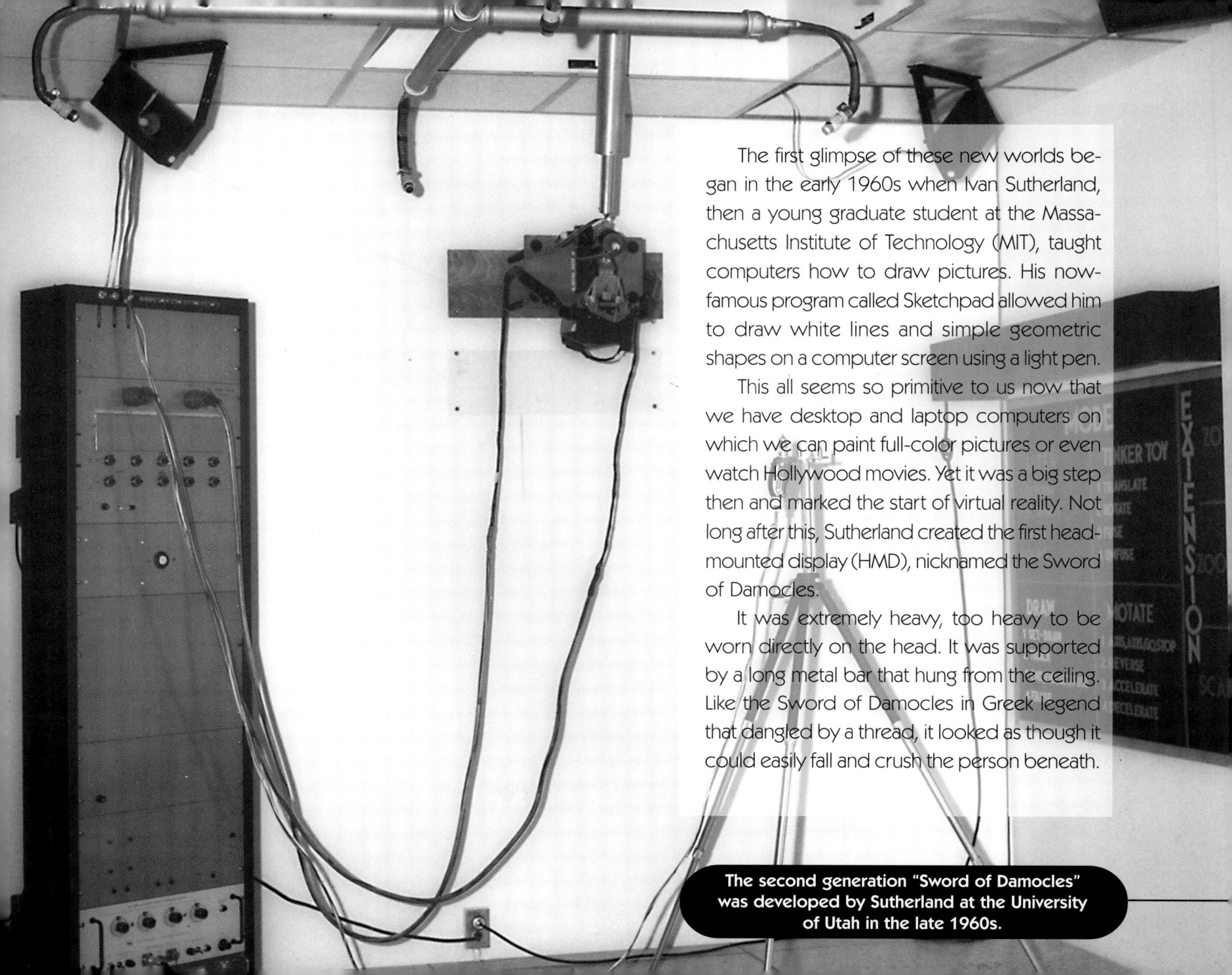

The first glimpse of these new worlds began in the early 1960s when Ivan Sutherland, then a young graduate student at the Massachusetts Institute of Technology (MIT), taught computers how to draw pictures. His now-famous program called Sketchpad allowed him to draw white lines and simple geometric shapes on a computer screen using a light pen.

This all seems so primitive to us now that we have desktop and laptop computers on which we can paint full-color pictures or even watch Hollywood movies. Yet it was a big step then and marked the start of virtual reality. Not long after this, Sutherland created the first head-mounted display (HMD), nicknamed the Sword of Damocles.

It was extremely heavy, too heavy to be worn directly on the head. It was supported by a long metal bar that hung from the ceiling. Like the Sword of Damocles in Greek legend that dangled by a thread, it looked as though it could easily fall and crush the person beneath.

The second generation "Sword of Damocles" was developed by Sutherland at the University of Utah in the late 1960s.

THE BUG THAT ATE DAYTON

Another early VR effort began in the late 1970s at Wright-Patterson Air Force Base, in Dayton, Ohio, under the direction of Dr. Thomas Furness. With the development of more complicated jet fighters, air combat was becoming more and more difficult to manage. One of the primary difficulties was that pilots still had to check their gauges and weapons statuses by looking down at control panels, thus diverting their attention from battle. At the increasing speeds of the new jets and the growing deadliness of their weapons, this could mean instant destruction.

What the air force needed was a display system that would give the pilot all the information he needed without having to divert his attention. From this effort came what is known as the "Heads-up Display," where pilot information is projected directly on the inside of a pilot's visor or windshield.

From these early and somewhat clumsy-looking efforts, research spread to universities and companies around the world, finally growing into the global VR industry we know today.

Early HMDs were anything but elegant. This bug-eyed monster, developed for project Super Cockpit at Wright-Patterson Air Force Base, provided a wide panoramic display.

PLAYING THE FOOL

So what makes a virtual reality seem so real? No matter how close you put your face to the computer monitor, nor how tightly you

An artist's conception of the goal of project Super Cockpit. The pilot would be able to see his optimum flight path, plus enemy targets and other flight data.

Ordinary binoculars? Not a chance. You use these binoculars to focus on virtual worlds just as you would on the real world.

Using this tiltable stereoscopic workbench, it is possible to reach out and touch the world.

grasp the mouse or joystick, you still don't feel like you're actually on the other side of the computer screen.

To really feel that you are inside another reality, your senses of sight, hearing, and touch must somehow be tricked. The computer must create sensations that hide the outside world and fool your mind into believing in a completely illusory reality. To understand how this is done, we must first look briefly at how our primary senses work.

The digital hand touching the virtual menu allows the user to see herself in VR.

VR doesn't always require an HMD. Here the user wears a pair of stereo glasses in a simpler, much less immersive approach.

EYES ON THE REAL WORLD

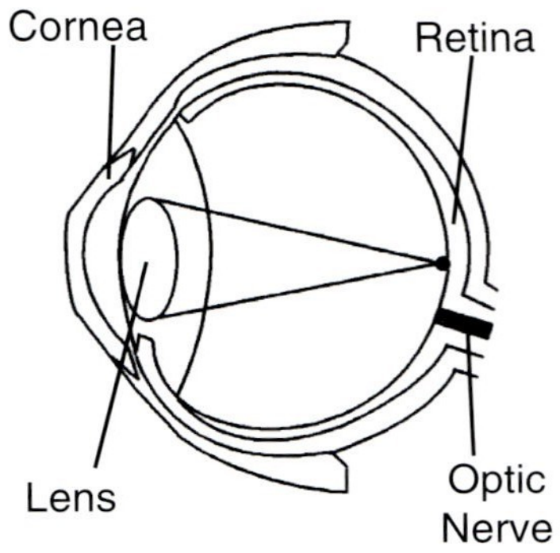

Sight is perhaps our most powerful way of gathering information about the world around us. We can see tiny details up close and great panoramas far away. We can see color, shadow, size, and depth, and from all this we can understand how close or distant any object is from us. Sight shows us how we fit inside the world around us.

For example, sitting at the dining table, you can look down at your fork and know exactly how far you need to move your hand to pick it up. You also know that when you look across a valley, you can't actually reach over and pick up the small-looking houses on the other side—even though it might be fun to imagine doing so.

How does all this happen? It is a combination of the structure of the eye and the placement of two of them at the front of our faces, looking in the same direction.

To sense color, brightness, and shadow, we have receptors known as rods and cones. The cones can see the colors red, green, and blue, while the rods see light and dark. To sense depth and distance, we use visual cues and our eye muscles themselves.

The simplest clue to determining distance is whether one object is in front of another. For example, a baseball pitcher knows the catcher is in front of the umpire because the catcher's body hides part of the umpire's body. And the pitcher sees that the batter is in front of the catcher because the batter's body hides part of the catcher's.

Parts of the eye

How the eye determines distance

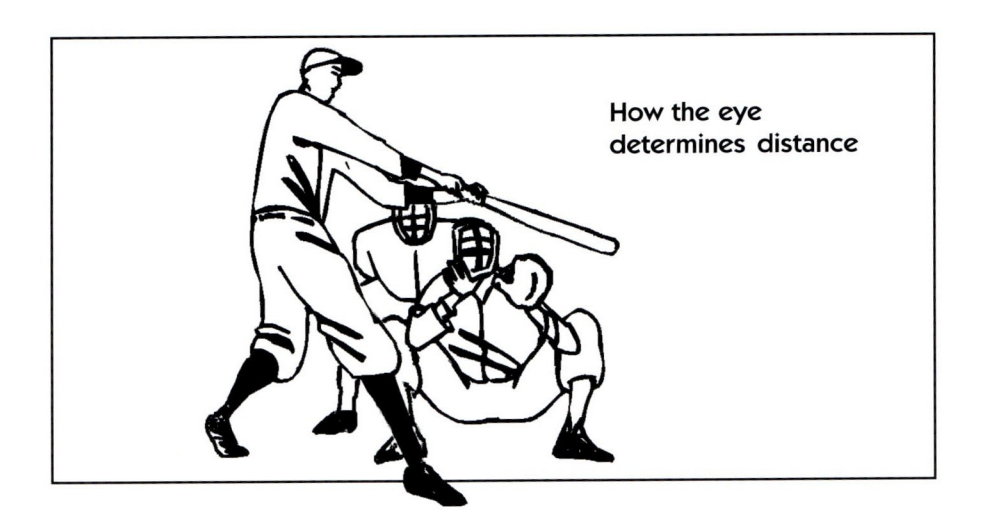

The physical focusing of the lens of the eye is another important way we can tell how far away something is. Close one eye for a moment, and focus on your hand with the open eye. Slowly move your hand closer and then farther away from your eye. Do you feel something changing in your eye? That feeling is the muscles of the lens making it thicker and thinner so your hand can stay in focus. This muscle movement sends a signal to the brain telling it how close or far something is from your eye.

Now open both eyes, and look around you. See how everything in the room—the table, the books, your friends—looks three-dimensional? What is it about your eyes that lets you see things this way? Why doesn't the world look flat like the view in cartoons?

Crossing Your Eyes

Your eyes' working together can also help you figure out how far away an object is. This time sit by a window, and look out as far as you can. After a few seconds focus on the inside windowsill. Then focus on the tip of your nose. Each time you focused your eyes on an object closer to you, your eyes turned inward toward each other until, when looking at your nose, they were as inward as they could go. This crossing of your eyes is another way your brain knows how to gauge just how distant something is.

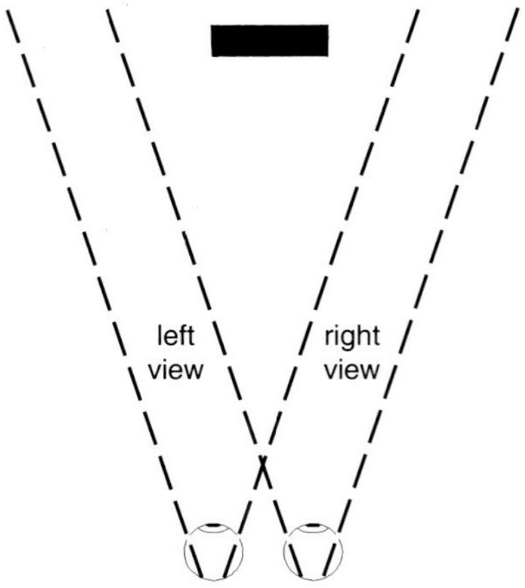

Stereopsis

The reason is that each eye sees a slightly different picture of what is in front of you. Once again raise your hand in front of you at arm's length, and stick your index finger in the air. Look at your finger. Now close one eye, and then open it while closing the other. Do this a few times slowly back and forth, and see how your finger appears to move.

These are the different views each eye has of your finger. When you use both eyes to look at the same object, your brain pastes these two views together and gives you a sense of depth, or stereo vision. With both eyes open, your finger looks fuller, rounder, and more real.

Of course, the workings of the eye are much more complicated than this, but you can at least start to get an idea of how you actually experience the world through vision.

EAR-TO-EAR REALITY

Hearing is the next most important sense for helping us feel a part of whatever reality we are in. Like sight, hearing helps us gauge the distance of sound-making objects, as well as their location, and gives us a feeling of the size of the space in which we happen to be.

The ear is far more than just what you see on the sides of people's heads. It contains not only the eardrum and the mechanisms for hearing sounds but also a fluid-filled inner ear that gives you your sense of balance. This inner ear is actually the source of one of the major problems with virtual reality—VR nausea—which we will talk about later.

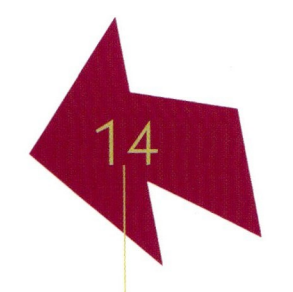

How sound is heard

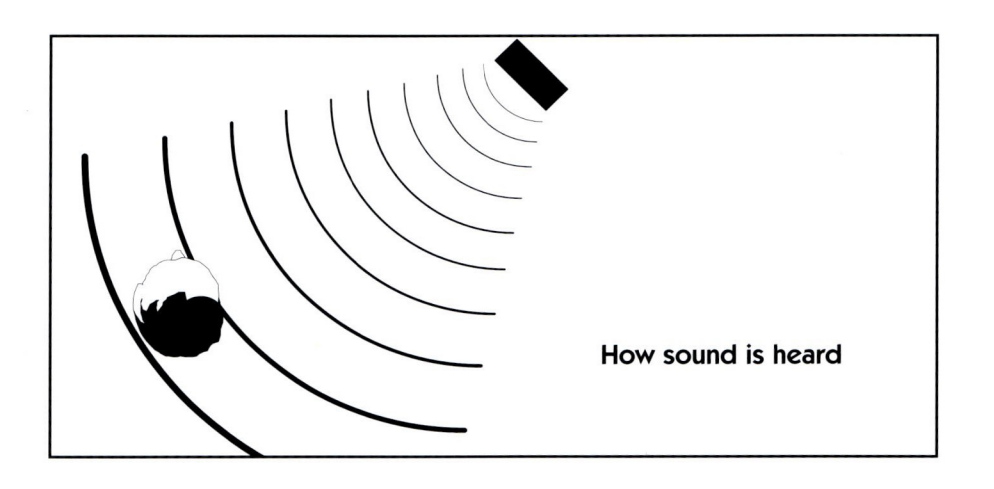

The location of sounds is a very important part of making sense of the world around you. Take a moment, and listen to the sounds that surround you. Perhaps you are reading this book in the library. Without looking up, you can hear sounds that are both close and far away, behind you or in front of you.

You might hear the clicking of a computer keyboard at the check-out desk or the rustling of a newspaper across the room. Because your ears know where the sounds are coming from, you know where to look when you glance up. What about the other kids talking softly at the table behind you? You turn around, and it is no surprise that they are there.

What helps you localize sounds in your world is your two ears and their placement on opposite sides of your head. Sound, as you may know, travels in invisible waves of pressure through the air from

Sound Sizing

Just to show you how hearing can affect your sense of the space around you, have someone blindfold you (or just close your eyes) and lead you into a small room in your house, perhaps a closet or a bathroom. Now shout and listen to how the small room sounds. Next, have them take you into a larger room, maybe the garage, and do the same thing. Notice the difference in the sound of the two spaces? Doesn't one "sound" larger than the other? This has to do with the length of time it takes for the sound waves from your shout to hit the walls around you and return to your ears.

the noise source, such as a radio, to your ears. Since your ears are on opposite sides of your head, the sound will usually be louder in the ear closest to the radio, in this case. In addition, the sound waves will reach the ear nearest to the radio first. They then hit the farther ear a brief moment later. You may not notice this difference, but your brain is aware of it.

Close your eyes, and stand approximately eight feet away from a radio or TV that is switched on. Now turn your body slowly, and see what happens to the sound. You should hear it shift to one side, go behind you, and then come back around the other side. Stop when you think you are facing the radio or TV directly.

When you open your eyes, you will most likely find you are facing in the right direction. This is because your brain is telling you that the volume of the sound in each ear is the same, and the sound waves are now hitting each ear at exactly the same time. This is possible only if you are directly facing the sound source.

IN TOUCH WITH REALITY

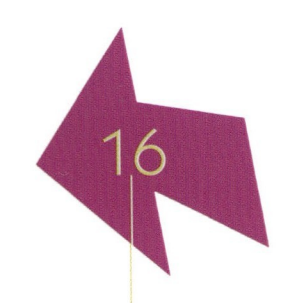

Touch also tells us a lot about the world we live in. We can sense touch anywhere on our skin, but we mostly associate it with our hands and fingers, because these are the parts of our body we most often use to contact the reality we live in.

Touch tells us if a carpet is rough or smooth, that water is wet, and that an edge of a knife is sharp or dull. It can also tell us if the

Gamemaker Namco Ltd., creates the sense of immersion in a virtual world by involving the player's entire body. The user rocks the mechanical horse forward and back to run down the straightaways, while using the reins to avoid other horses and the rail.

wind is blowing, whether our hair feels long or short, and if our old pair of sneakers still fits. Touch, combined with the sensation of our muscles flexing as we lift something, lets us know how heavy a brick is or how strongly two magnets are attracting each other.

The sensation of having contact with an object in the space around you, such as the book you are now holding, gives the world an important sense of solidity and permanence.

FROM REAL TO VIRTUAL:

STEPPING THROUGH THE SCREEN

A high-resolution BOOM display is used to explore a computer restoration of the 14th century Basilica of St. Francis of Assisi in Italy.

Now you can begin to see some of the difficulties in creating a virtual world that is believable. You need to see things as you see them in the real world. That is, the objects need to have depth and distance, shadows, and, ideally, colors. And your eyes need to be able to focus at will on objects that appear both near and far.

Sounds need to come from the objects that make the noises and not to shift around as we move. In other words, the music coming from a virtual radio must always appear to come from that radio and not from a chair, door, wall, or whatever we happen to be facing. And finally, objects that look solid must also feel and act solid when we touch them.

These are all difficult problems to overcome. Not only must complex hardware such as head-mounted displays, touch devices, and sound systems be created and worn on various parts of the body but a detailed VR world also requires an immense amount of computing power to make it seem real. In fact, the most convincing virtual realities require the massive computing power of a modern supercomputer.

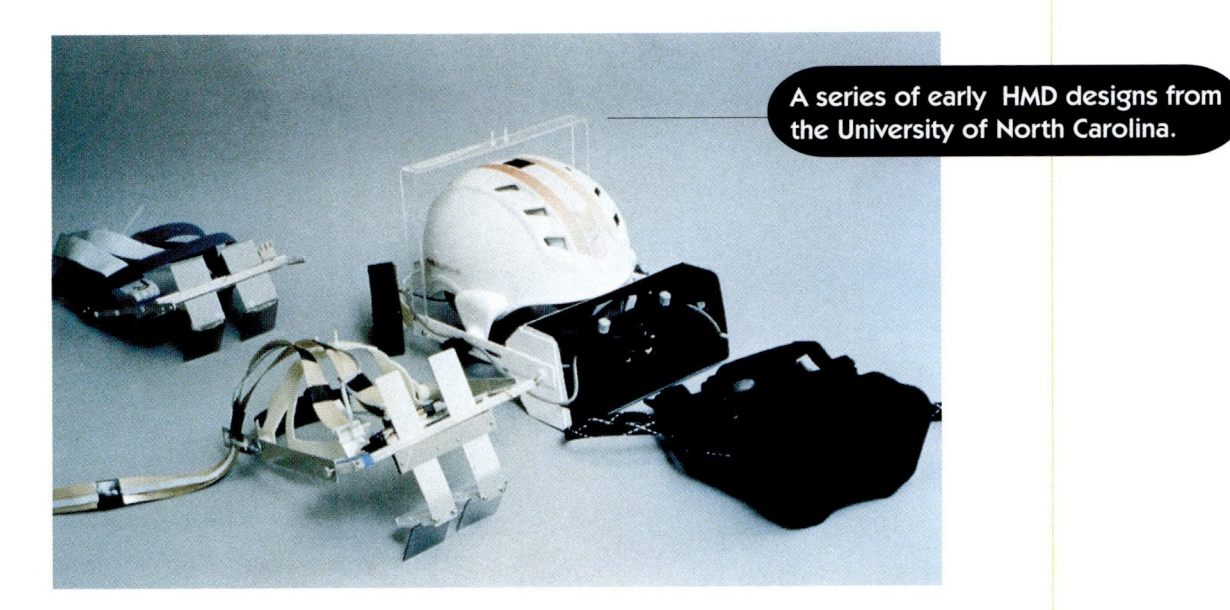

A series of early HMD designs from the University of North Carolina.

SEEING IS BELIEVING

Since the eyes are the most important sense for gathering information about the world, scientists developing virtual reality focused first on head-mounted displays. All current HMDs share the same qualities: They cut off all views of the outside world (except in "augmented realities," which we will touch on later), they use special lenses that increase the field of view (how wide an area you can see), and they provide separate views for each eye to imitate our normal sense of stereo vision.

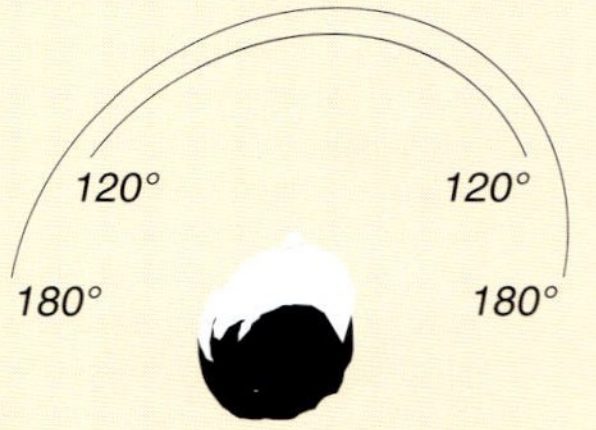

Field of View

Sit for a moment, and look straight ahead. Without moving your eyes to either side, become aware of all that you can see. Not only can you see what you are looking at but you are also aware of much of your surroundings on either side. This is called peripheral vision. If you now move your eyes as far as you can to either side without turning your head, you can even see a little bit in back of you. This entire span of vision is called your field of view and is greater than 180 degrees. The largest field of view today's HMDs provide is about 120 degrees. But this is still wide enough to seem like the real thing.

Once a display system is built in the form of an HMD, a virtual world must be created. This can be built using several different software products geared for the development of virtual worlds. Whatever package is used, 3D graphics must be created. (2D graphics are like most Saturday morning cartoons and are called 2D, or two dimensional, because they are flat. 3D graphics, on the other hand, look more like the real world, because objects have size and depth, and you can move around them.)

THE VIEW FROM INSIDE

Let's assume we have completed these first steps of creating a virtual world and developing an HMD. It is now time to try it. You put on your headset. It can weigh as much as three pounds, but it balances well and fits snugly. Then you turn on the world. There it is before you, ready to be explored! You can't wait. But very quickly you realize something is terribly wrong. How can you get around? There is no mouse, and your hands are outside the HMD and not visible at all.

You have just discovered the need for two very important VR components: a tracking system to let you know where you are inside the VR world and a way to interact with that world.

Tracking systems of one form or another are essential for creating realistic experiences in virtual realities. What they do is to tell the computer how you are moving, so that it can then change what you are seeing in your HMD. In the real world, for example, if you tilt your head or turn to look over your shoulder, your view of the world automatically changes around you.

This same thing should happen inside your virtual world. Based on what the tracking system tells the computer, it then changes your virtual view through a series of complex and extremely rapid image calculations.

Many different kinds of tracking systems have been created, the most common of which use magnetic fields and sensors. VR users, or "cybernauts," as some people call them, wear a selection of magnetic sensors on various parts of the body, such as the head, hands, arms, or legs, depending on the system's complexity.

Next the person steps into a large magnetic field. The interaction of the magnetic field with the wearable sensors tells the computer how the users are tilting their head or moving their arms and legs. This

To move inside his virtual world, this soldier pushes the pedals mounted on the pedestal.

VR Worlds Are Pretty Simple

Virtual worlds are still grossly simplified versions of our normal reality. Virtual trees do not have countless different leaves nor are VR lawns composed of millions of blades of grass. This is because each separate detail in a virtual reality increases the number of calculations a computer must execute in order to create the visual image.

Even the fastest computer today can only handle a limited number of these calculations in real time. While the level of detail in virtual realities has increased tremendously over the last few years, it will be a long time before we can experience the incredible, rich variety available in the real world. But while VR worlds are simple, they are far from easy.

Virtual reality is not always a picnic. A VR model of Fort Ord in California proved very difficult to navigate without getting lost, even with a compass. This is because the level of detail possible in VR is still quite low. The greater the detail, the easier it is to remember landmarks.

movement information is then sent to the computer, which rapidly changes what is seen in the HMD.

BECOMING VISIBLE

Go back inside the virtual world again. With the tracker working, you can now turn around, look up and down, and even squat to look under objects nearby. But there is still no convenient way to travel through and to interact with what is out there. This is because right now only your eyes are inside the virtual world, via the HMD.

In the real world, you can look down and see your body. You can see your hand reach out and grab a pencil from the desk in front of you. But in VR your body is missing. What do you do? How do you get inside with your body as well as your eyes? To do so, you'll need to add even more hardware to what you are already wearing.

The most common piece of VR apparel is the fiber-optic glove. This glove is made out of soft, flexible fabric and has several small fiber-optic cables sewn onto the tops of all the fingers and across the back of the hand. Signals are sent down these fiber-optic channels telling the computer how your fingers are flexing or straightening.

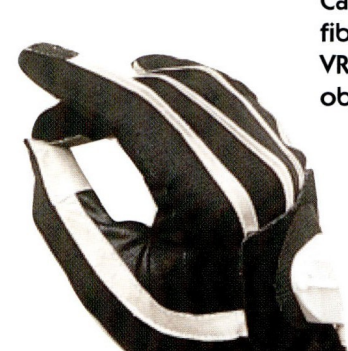

Called PINCH gloves, these fiber-optic-lined gloves help VR users grab and manipulate objects in their virtual worlds.

With this information the computer can then show you computer-graphic models of your own hands opening and closing or pointing and relaxing inside the virtual reality. Coupled with the motion sensors you are wearing, the fiber-optic glove allows you to see what your hands are doing and where they are moving.

Researchers have also developed entire fiber-optic bodysuits, which allow cybernauts to see computer images of their whole bodies in action. For most uses of VR today, however, bodysuits are not necessary. An engineer designing a car-instrument panel in virtual reality, for example, really only needs to see her hands to test how convenient and workable her design is.

GOING MOBILE

Now that you can see yourself, or at least your hands, you are ready to explore and interact with your new environment. The simplest way to get around inside a VR is by pointing and flying. VRs that use the glove-based approach have developed a series of gestures that mean certain things to the computer.

Taking the typical baby walker into virtual reality, the Naval Postgraduate School created the Perambulator to help users to move around in cyberspace.

For example, if you point in a given direction, the computer will assume that you want to go there and will fly you forward until you stop pointing. Depending on your software, other gestures could bring down menus of selected actions or let you pick up a virtual object and move it.

A student at Iowa State University uses a bicycle hooked to a two-walled CAVE to explore a virtual model of the university grounds.

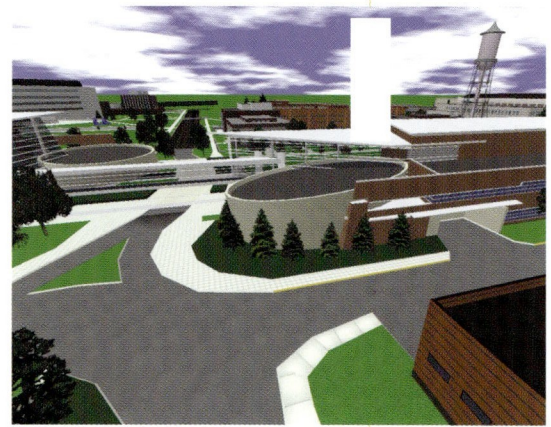

25

Help, I'm Going to Be Sick!

Although it sounds like fun, moving around in virtual reality, no matter how you do it, can cause problems. In fact, many people often feel very nauseated. It's strange: We don't feel sick moving around in the real world, and VR tries to imitate the real world as closely as possible. What could be the problem?

Let's say you decide to fly through your VR world. You point, and off you go—up, down, and around. Your eyes see that you are flying; your mind might even give you a giddy feeling of takeoff. Yet your body's real balance system, located in the inner ear, is still sensing that it is standing on the ground or sitting in a chair.

It is this split in perception that is the heart of the problem. Your mind gets caught in between and so signals that something is wrong by making you feel nauseated.

Flying, while exhilarating, is often not the best way to get around in certain VR systems, particularly if you are testing something like a building design or wanting to train foot soldiers in combat situations. In these cases you might prefer to feel as though you are traveling on foot.

Researchers at the University of North Carolina at Chapel Hill created a steerable treadmill to explore their new computer-science building before it was even built. As cybernauts walked on the treadmill, the computer sensed how far the treadmill had moved and changed what the people were seeing just as if they were walking forward.

In stepping through the detailed computer model of their new building, scientists actually discovered that a hallway area was too narrow and would create traffic jams as students tried to change classes. The architect was alerted, and corrected the problem before the building was constructed, saving thousands of dollars in later remodeling costs.

Similarly, scientists at the Naval Postgraduate School in Monterey, California, developed what they called an omnidirectional treadmill for their work with foot soldiers. Normal treadmills only operate in one line of motion, forward and backward. The omnidirectional (meaning all directions) treadmill can move side to side as well. Soldiers using this virtual-reality motion system can move quickly and easily in any direction across virtual terrain just as if they were in live combat situations.

A computer-generated image of Sitterson Hall before construction. This computer model was used for a virtual walkthrough of the building before it was built.

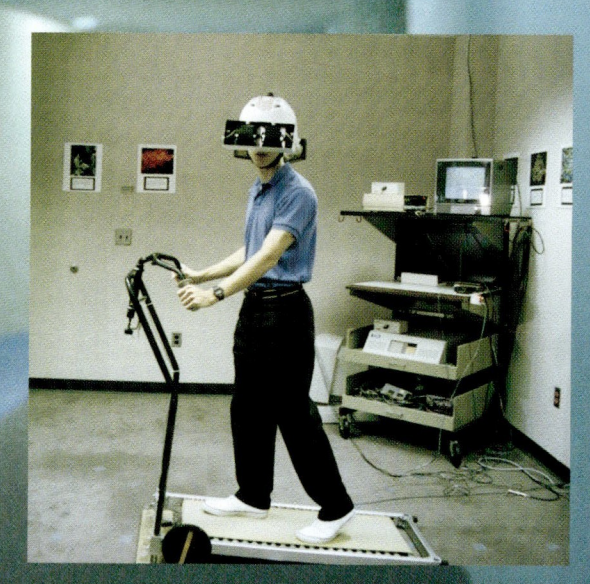

UNC graduate student John Airey uses a steerable treadmill to walk through the computer model of Sitterson Hall. This process was used to spot and correct a problem in the building's design.

The real thing: UNC's Sitterson Hall after construction.

V-DESK

This giant curved screen display system allows several people at once to immerse themselves in a virtual world without the need for cumbersome head-mounted displays.

TRIMENSION ▶ Virtual system integrators

SOUNDS GREAT

Now that you can see yourself and move around inside your virtual reality, let's make it even more real. Let's add sound and some sense of physical contact.

As we mentioned before, three-dimensional sound is around us all the time. It is quite different from simple stereophonic sound that you can hear through a set of CD-player headphones. Stereo sound certainly puts you in the middle of the music, but it doesn't change at all when you move your head from one position to another.

To create such a system in virtual reality, it is essential that you also use a head-position tracker, as mentioned earlier. In this case the computer will use the head-tracking information to change what you see, and it will also alter what you hear.

Do you remember that sound reaches each ear at a different time, depending on where the sound source is located? The computer can exactly duplicate that effect by slightly changing the audio signals sent to each earphone as you move your head in cyberspace. Thus, if you start out facing a virtual alarm clock that is ringing and then turn to the right, the computer will send the sound signal to your left ear slightly before it goes to your right ear. It will also change the volume for each ear. The alarm will sound a bit quieter in the ear that is moving away from it.

HEAR ME TOUCH THIS

Finally, you need to be able actually to touch and feel the objects surrounding you in virtual reality. The sensation of feeling the objects around you is so natural in our everyday world that we hardly think about it, yet this sensation is very difficult to translate to the virtual world.

Take a moment to think about it. How can something created by a computer, that has absolutely no physical substance whatso-ever, act like something in the physical world? How, when you push on a virtual object, will it provide the resistance you are used to? How can you grab it and not simply squeeze your fingers right through it?

These are all difficult questions to answer and have been the subject of long and continuing testing and research. One of the early approaches that was surprisingly effective was the use of sound to indicate contact with a virtual object. For example, if you reached out with your virtual hand to pick up a virtual skateboard, you would hear a tone or a beep. You would know then that you had the skateboard in your grasp and could move it around.

This form of sound substitution works well in many cases and is still in use, but it is far from satisfactory. The most realistic thing would be actually to feel some sort of return force or pressure when you make contact with something in a virtual world.

HAPTICS ARE HAPPENING

Haptics? What a strange word. Its root meaning comes from Ancient Greek and relates to the sensation of touch. In current VR research, haptic technology refers to all the devices used to create a sense of touch, or what is called "force feedback."

A whole variety of such devices have been invented, but the most effective to date have been either extensive metal exoskeletons (external frameworks) that are worn on the hands, arms, or body or more delicate desktop touch devices that are either worn on a fingertip or held in the hand like a pen. All these devices are wired with sensors to register their movements, as well as various motion inhibitors to create resistance when a virtual object is contacted.

For example, a mechanical arm was created at the University of North Carolina and used to help chemists study various molecules in virtual reality. The chemist would strap on the arm and then look at a large screen projection of a particular molecule. He could then use the arm actually to touch and manipulate the virtual molecule. If he wanted to try to connect that molecule to another or take the molecule apart, he could feel the atomic forces either repelling or attracting at different places on the molecule.

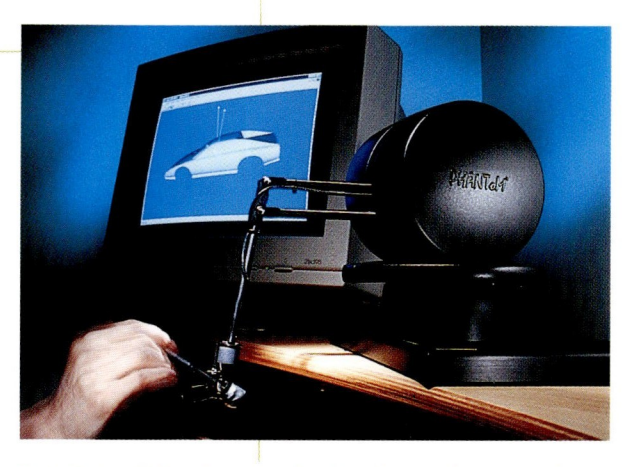

This PHANTOM haptic device is used to touch the computer world directly. As the user moves the penlike pointer, he can actually feel the surface of the object on the screen, in this case a car body.

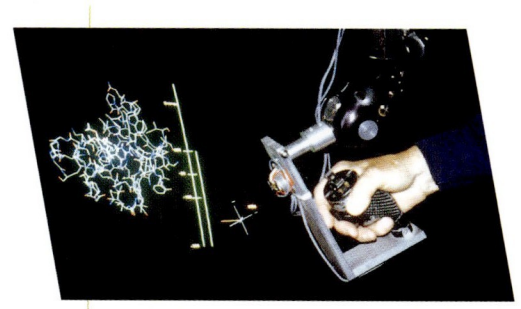

A close-up of the handgrip of UNC's force-feedback device.

31

The sense of touch, or force feedback, has also been used in various arcade games since the late 1980s. In many road-race games the strength required to turn a car's steering wheel changes depending on whether you are driving on the road or have skidded off the track.

In general, haptic devices are still too cumbersome and expensive to be used regularly in most virtual-reality applications. But, like everything else in the field of high technology, this is changing faster than we can imagine. Someday soon we may literally be able to get in "touch" with others instead of simply calling them on the phone.

WHY VIRTUAL?

Now that you know what it takes to make a full-blown virtual-reality system, perhaps we should ask "Why bother?" The answers to this question vary as much as do the people who use the technology. Engineers see VR as a way to more quickly design, create prototypes for, and even test new products before they are actually built. Scientists see VR as a way to climb inside and better understand their data, whether they are examining the interaction of molecules or the collisions of galaxies. Medical doctors use VR to help plan complex operations or to "see" inside their patients' bodies without surgery. And entertainment designers view this exciting field as a means of providing experiences that either don't exist or that might be too dangerous in real life.

THE MANY FACES OF VR

Even though we have examined the basic components of a typical VR system, virtual reality actually comes in many shapes and sizes. A head-mounted display is not the only way to create a virtual reality. The Electronic Visualization Lab at the University of Chicago pioneered quite a different VR system, which they named the CAVE.

A CAVE is actually a room-size box with projection screens on each side of the room. The space inside is large enough to hold several people at once for a shared VR experience. Computer-created images are then projected onto the surrounding screens, making the participants truly feel they are inside the computer. A navigation device in the form of an electronic pointer allows those present to move around inside the data being shown.

For example, if an automobile is being crash-tested in virtual reality, three or four engineers can watch the process together from any angle, even from inside the car itself, without fear of being hurt.

Four people play a game inside a two-walled CAVE. Note the virtual hand. It is the digital representation of the hand of the person wearing the fiber-optic glove.

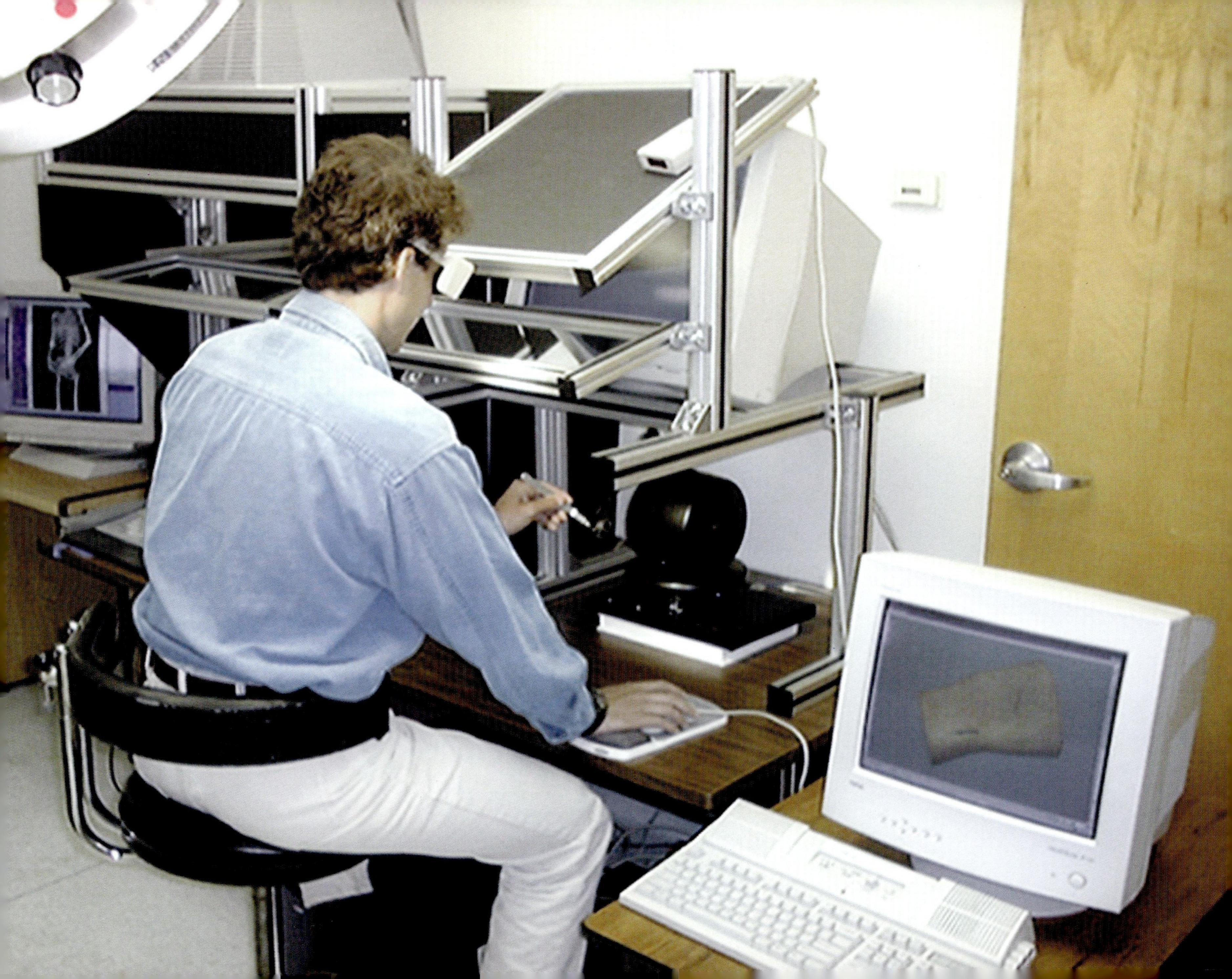

VIRTUAL MEDICINE

Because of the incredible complexity of many areas of surgery, the medical field is making increasing use of virtual reality as a surgical planning and training tool. The University of Colorado Center for Human Simulation has developed the most detailed virtual models of human male and female bodies and has also invented a virtual surgical training system.

Looking into the VR world of this surgical training system, you can see the image of a human knee. Holding the desktop haptic device called PHANTOM, you can look at the virtual image and see that you are holding a life-size scalpel. Taking the scalpel and drawing it across the virtual tissue of the knee, you can feel a sense of drag as the blade cuts the skin. If you happen to make a mistake and cut too deep, you can feel a jarring contact with the bone beneath and even see the bone as the cut widens. Fortunately, the patient is only virtual and will not suffer from your lack of skill.

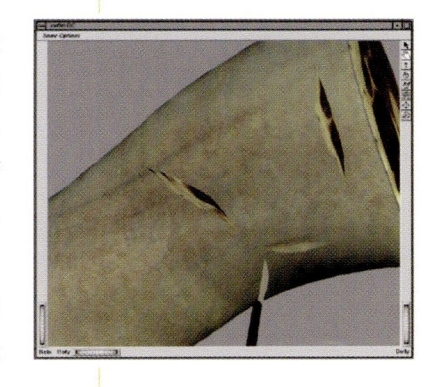

Facing page: A researcher at the University of Colorado Center for Human Simulation seems to work on nothing at all. What he sees and feels is a virtual scalpel cutting into a virtual knee (above).

AUGMENTED REALITY

What would you think of owning a pair of X-ray glasses that can see through someone's skin to the bones beneath? Or, what if you had a pair of glasses with one lens flashing information to you about anything you wanted? School tests would be a breeze.

Such devices, though largely experimental, do exist today. Doctors at Brigham and Women's Hospital in Boston in conjunction with scientists from MIT are working on perfecting real X-ray-like glasses to aid surgeons during delicate surgery. Here's how it works: The doctor performing surgery wears a different kind of head-mounted display than we described earlier. In this case, she is able to see the outside world through the lenses. However, the lenses, because they are partially reflective, are also able to show the doctor a computer-created image superimposed on her patient.

For example, if the doctor is trying to remove a tumor deep inside a patient's brain, she would be able to see not only the patient's head, but a computer-made image of the brain inside the skull and the target tumor inside the brain. In addition, she would be able to see her instruments as they work around the tumor.

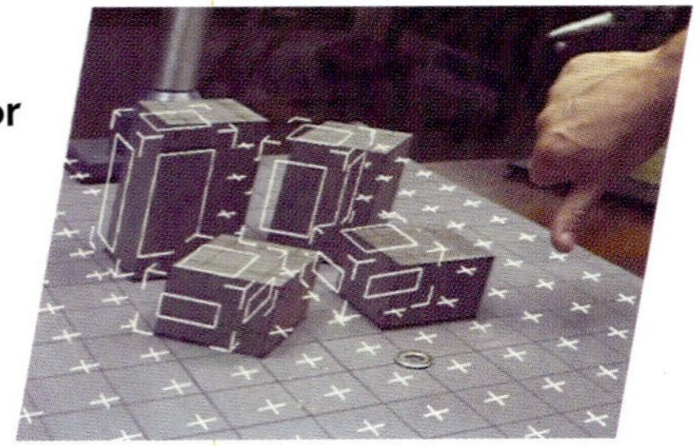

There are still many very serious difficulties to overcome before this approach to surgery becomes an everyday reality. One, for example, is ensuring that the computer image always stays at exactly the right place on a patient's body, no matter how the doctor or the patient moves. If the positioning were to slip even slightly, the surgeon might mistakenly cut in the wrong area. For this reason these systems are still very experimental, but they are destined to be available in the years to come.

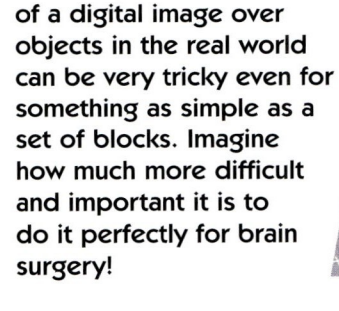

Achieving the perfect overlay of a digital image over objects in the real world can be very tricky even for something as simple as a set of blocks. Imagine how much more difficult and important it is to do it perfectly for brain surgery!

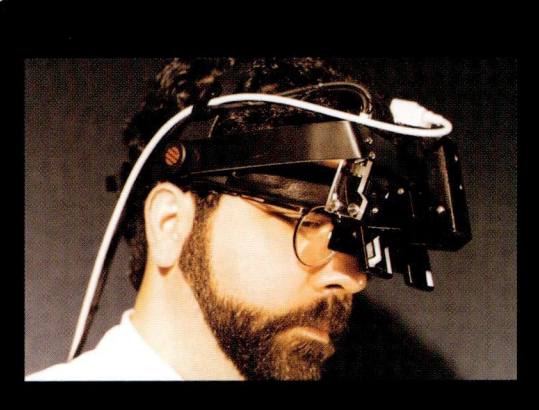

Left: Dr. David Casalino wears a video see-through HMD for his research on the uses of augmented reality in medicine. Right and below: Doctors at Brigham and Women's Hospital, together with researchers from MIT, have created an augmented reality system to aid in brain surgery. Here we see a patient without a digital overlay, with a partial digital overlay, and finally with a full digital overlay of data obtained through a magnetic resonance imaging (MRI) scan of her brain.

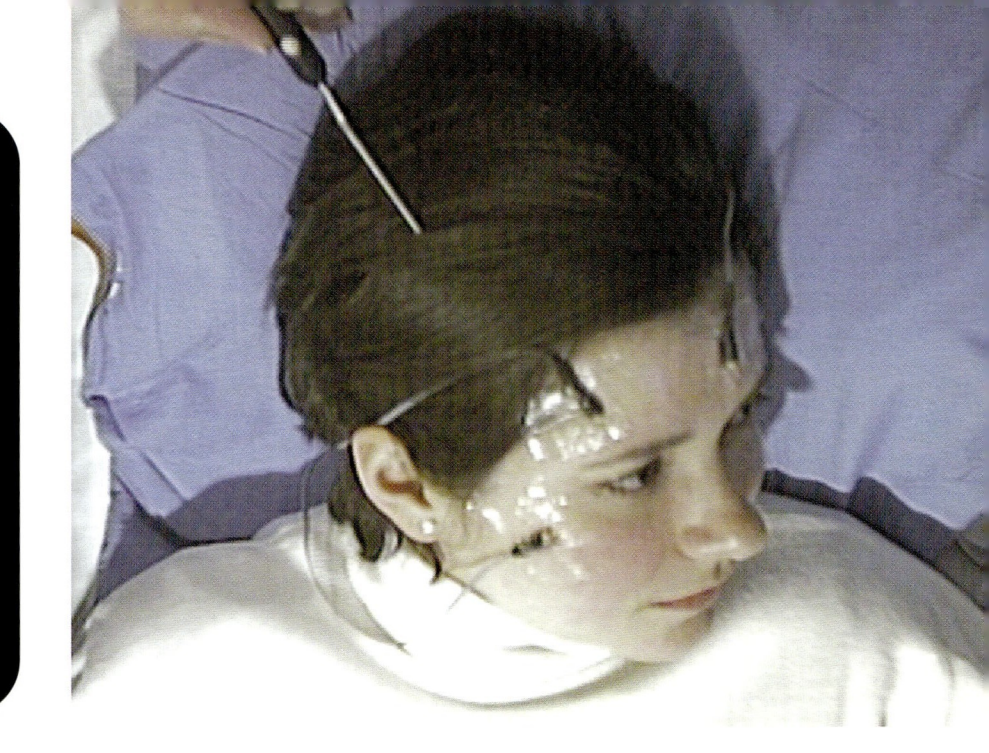

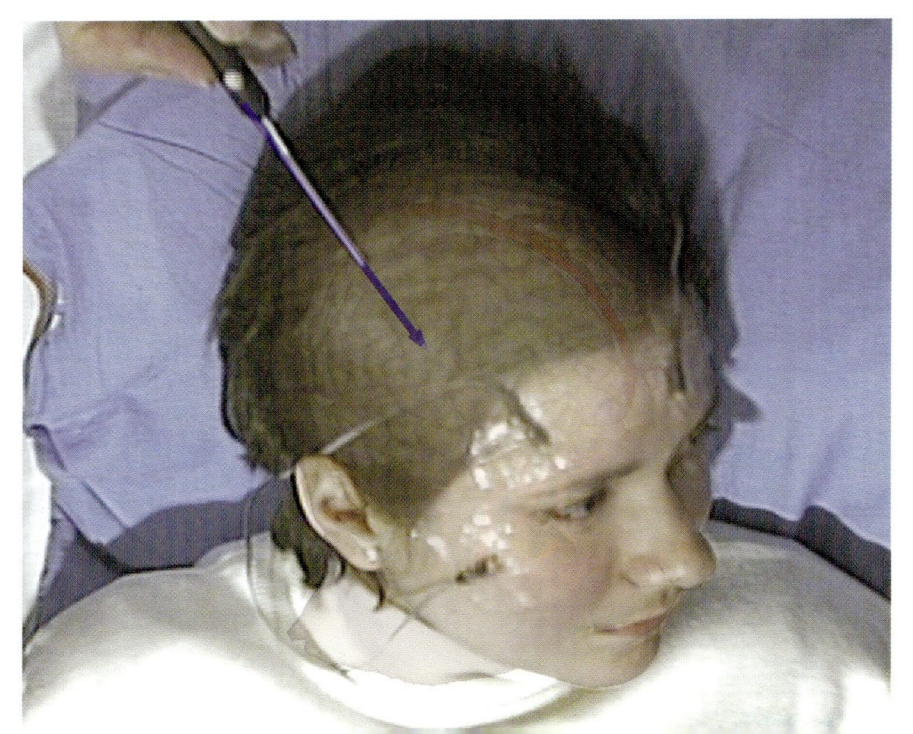

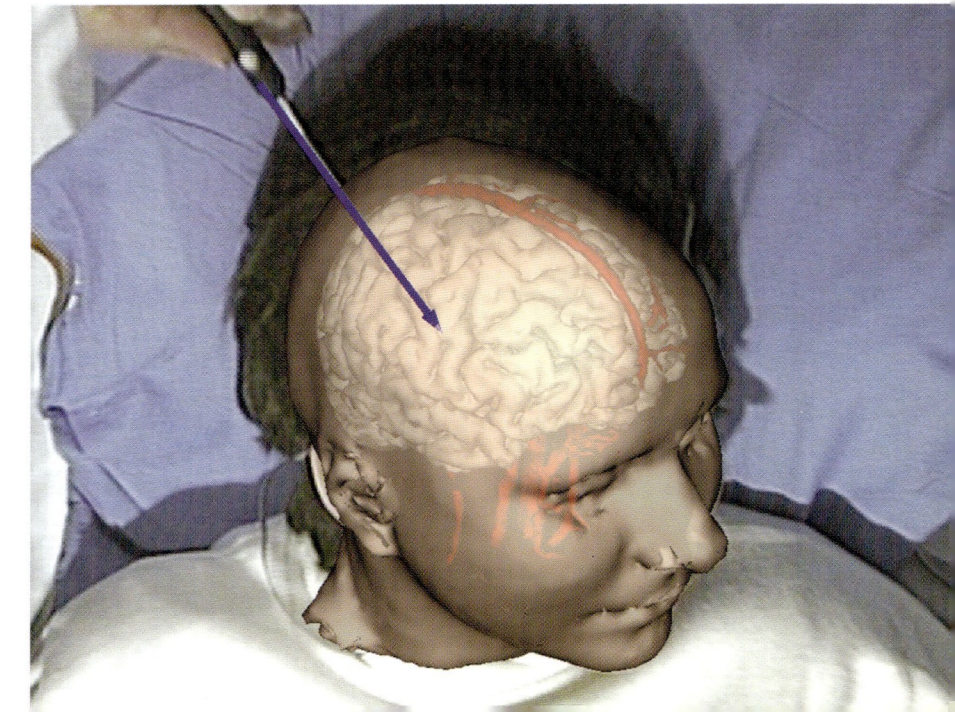

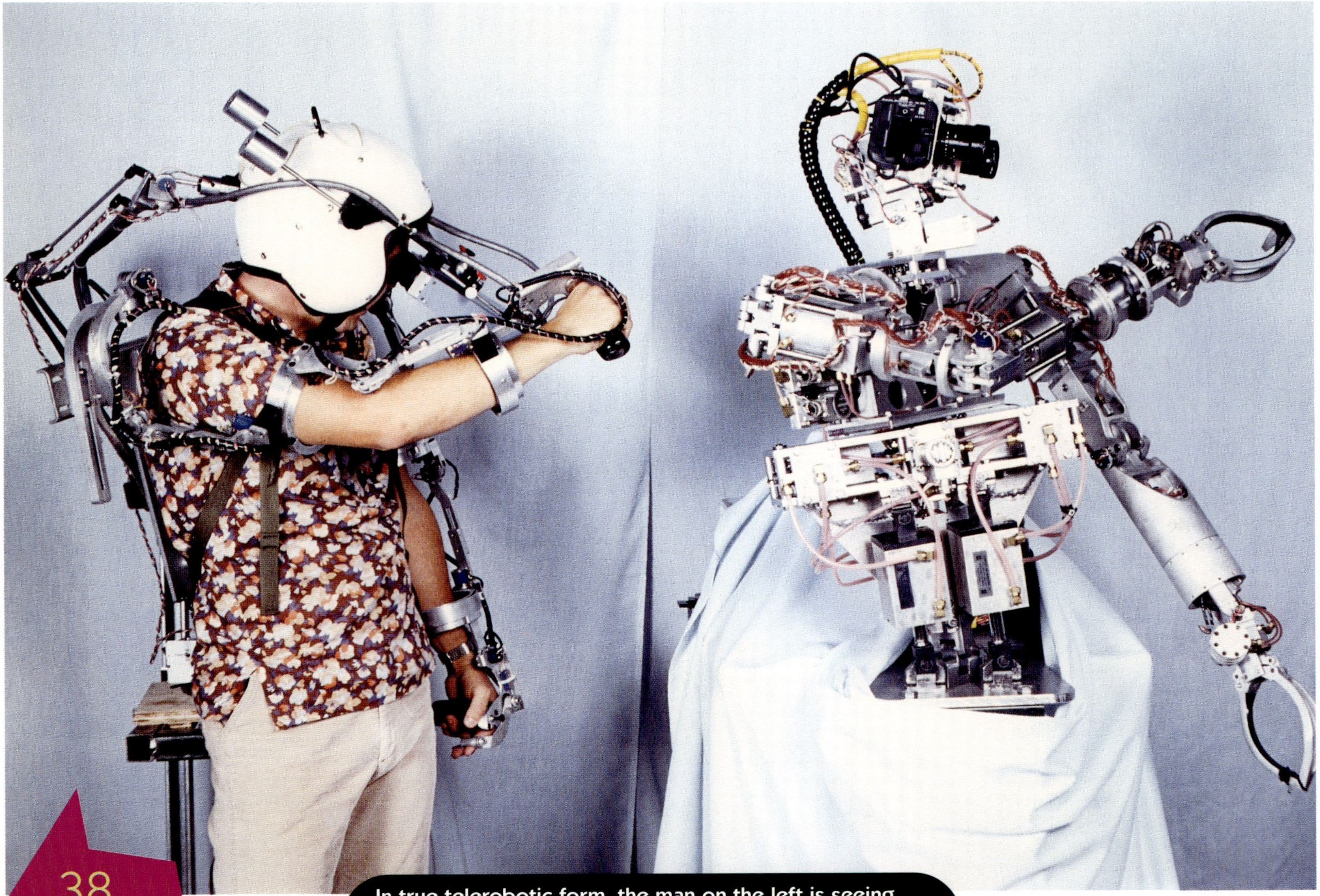

In true telerobotic form, the man on the left is seeing what the robot on the right sees, and the robot is turning and moving exactly as the man turns and moves.

38

WANT TO BE IN TWO PLACES
AT ONCE? TRY TELEROBOTICS

When was the last time you were in two places at the same time? Likely never, unless you happened to experience the related field of telerobotics. The prefix "tele" comes from Ancient Greek and means "at a distance." Television views things from a distance. Telerobotics entails operating robots from a distance.

The gear, hardware, and software used to make telerobotics work are essentially the same as those used for virtual reality. In this case, though, what you see in your HMD is not a computer-created reality but video images of a different part of the real world as seen through the "eyes" of the robot you are controlling.

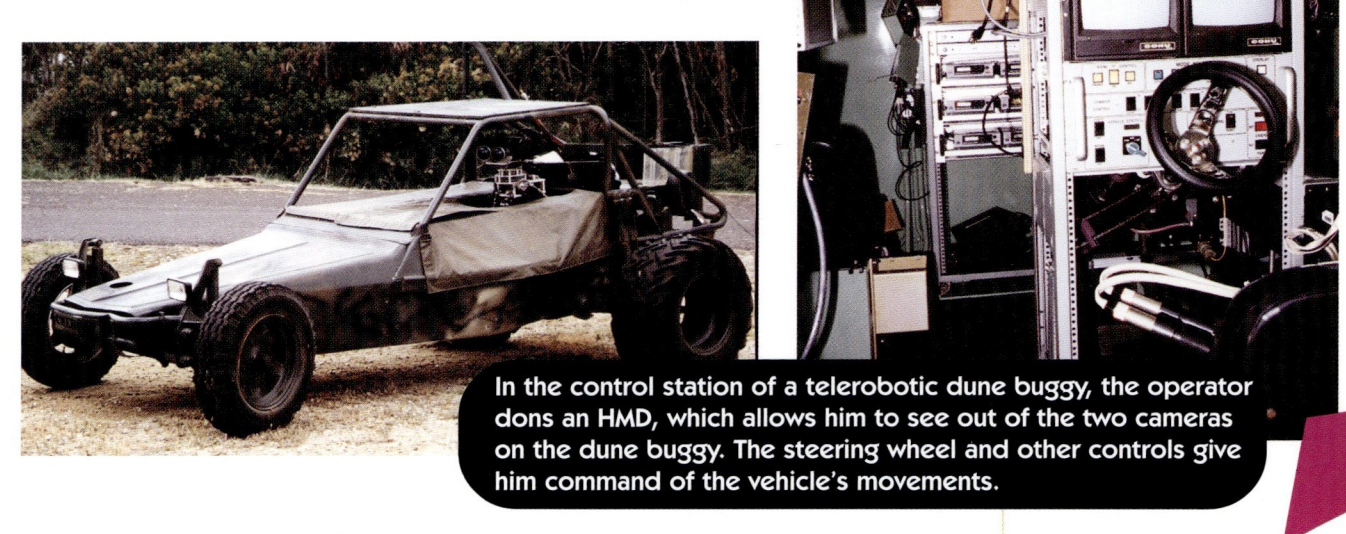

In the control station of a telerobotic dune buggy, the operator dons an HMD, which allows him to see out of the two cameras on the dune buggy. The steering wheel and other controls give him command of the vehicle's movements.

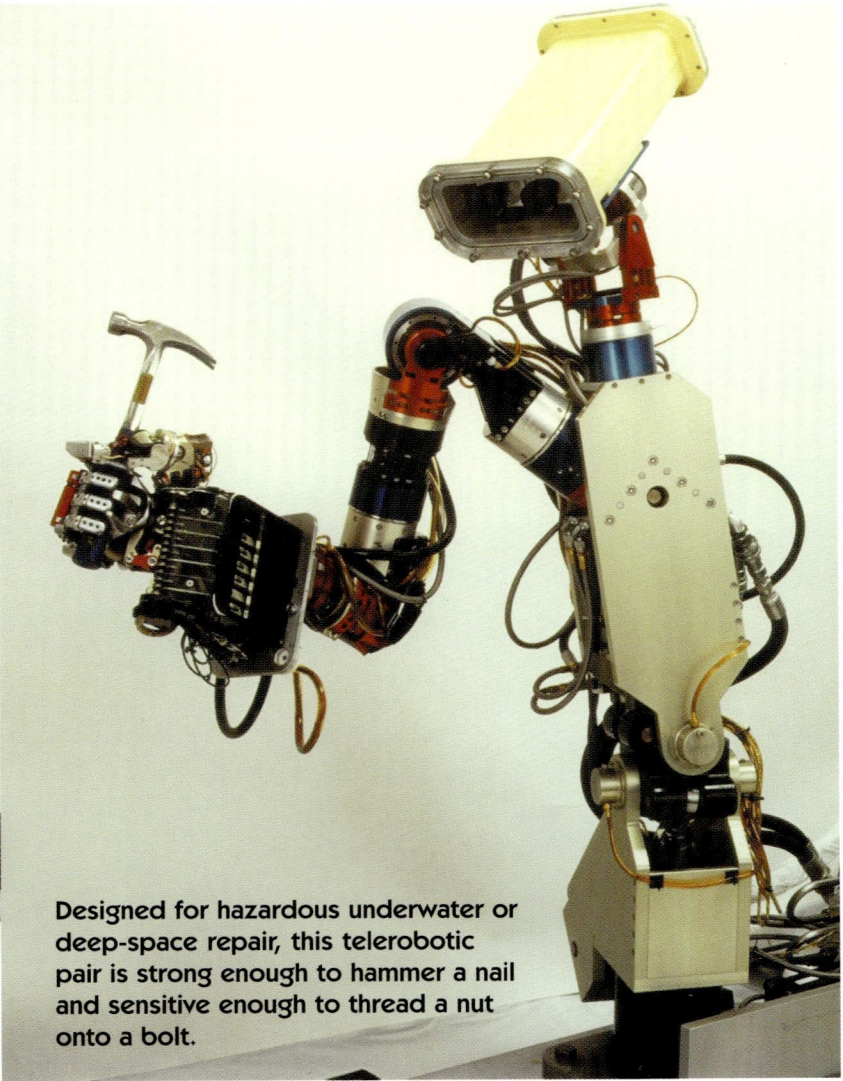

Designed for hazardous underwater or deep-space repair, this telerobotic pair is strong enough to hammer a nail and sensitive enough to thread a nut onto a bolt.

40

Telerobots come in all shapes and sizes. Some are flat-topped with wheels, like NASA's Sojourner rover, used in the Mars Pathfinder mission. Some are round and can become airborne, like the surveillance fliers built by the Naval Ocean Systems Center in Hawaii. Still others are shaped like humans and are designed for human tasks in exploring such hazardous environments as deep under the sea or in outer space.

Whatever the case, when an operator dons the HMD, he sees what the robot is seeing. And when he wears the exoskeleton—in cases where it is necessary—he feels via force feedback what the robot is touching. Some telerobots have such refined senses of touch that they can even pick up eggs without breaking them or screw in light-bulbs without shattering the glass.

A VIRTUAL FUTURE

The truth is, we have barely begun to see what VR can do for us. Think of the telephone or television. There is hardly a home in the United States that doesn't have at least one of each. We use them to keep in touch with those we know and to learn about the world around us.

Imagine now, instead of calling your friends, actually meeting them in cyberspace in worlds of your own choosing. Or, if you need to learn something about a particular place in the world or a time in

Imagine you've been given a school assignment to do a report on the Roman Pantheon. With virtual reality you could "step inside" a computer reconstruction of the building and see what it is really like.

history, you can go there via virtual reality and thus get a more complete understanding of its flavor.

Think, too, of space exploration. Already we are sending robots to other planets, something that many have argued we should have been doing long before we sent humans to space. It's cheaper and easier and if disaster strikes, only money and time are lost, not lives. NASA's Mars Pathfinder mission was such an extraordinary success that a series of other planetary robot missions have been scheduled to follow.

Going for a virtual test drive. VR systems such as this two-walled CAVE at Iowa State University's Virtual Reality Applications Center (VRAC) give researchers a chance to test new automobile control designs before the cars are built.

And what about science itself? How will it be affected by VR? It is likely that the current rapid rate of discovery will accelerate even more. When a scientist can see and physically manipulate her data in a virtual space, her understanding of the problems she is studying increases greatly. This greater understanding can then lead to a breakthrough discovery. In the near future, with the aid of VR, we can expect to see further into the mysteries of the universe, of atomic structure, and of the human body than ever before.

And, of course, there will be new forms of entertainment that go well beyond the current virtual-reality theme-park rides. Perhaps we will share adventures over the Internet, join others in large VR theaters where we can participate in a worldwide virtual Olympics, or even play roles alongside the stars in the latest Hollywood VR movies.

Whatever happens, one thing is certain: Virtual reality will play a key part in expanding our understanding of the actual reality in which we live and our world.

RESOURCES

There are literally hundreds of sites on the Web that deal with virtual reality in its various forms. So get out there and explore with the aid of your favorite internet search engine. To get you started, here is a small number of leading research Web sites.

Iowa State University, Virtual Reality Applications Center (VRAC)
www.vrac.iastate.edu/

University of Washington, Human Interface Technology Lab (HITL)
www.hitl.washington.edu/

National Center for Supercomputer Applications (NCSA) VR lab
www.ncsa.uiuc.edu/VR/VR/VRHomePage.html

Stanford University, Center for Design Research, Virtual Space Exploration Lab and related telepresence projects
cdr.stanford.edu/html/telepresence/

Johnson Space Center, Virtual Environment Technology Laboratory
www.vetl.uh.edu/

University of Chicago, Electronic Visualization Laboratory
www.evl.uic.edu/EVL/

University at Buffalo, Virtual Reality Laboratory
wings.buffalo.edu/academic/department/eng/mae/vrlab/

Georgia Tech, Virtual Environments Group
www.cc.gatech.edu/gvu/virtual/

University of North Carolina, Telepresence Research Group
www.cs.unc.edu/~mcmillan/telep.html

NASA Space Telerobotics Program
ranier.oact.hq.nasa.gov/telerobotics_page/telerobotics.shtm

Yahoo list of devices connected to the Internet
dir.yahoo.com/Computers_and_Internet/Internet/
Devices_Connected_to_the_Internet/

INDEX

Page numbers in *italics* refer to illustrations.

Airey, John, *27*
Arcade games, 32
Augmented reality, 19, 35–36, *37*

Balance, sense of, 14, 26
Binoculars, *10*
Bodysuits, 24
BOOM display, *18*
Brigham and Women's Hospital, Boston, 36, *37*
Brightness, 12

Casalino, David, 37
CAVE, 33, *33*, 43
Color, 12, 18
Combat situations, 8, 26
Computer Adventures computer camp, Washington State, *6*
Cones of eye, 12
Crossing eyes, 13
Cybernauts, 21, 24, 26

Depth, 12, 14, 18
Distance, 12, 18

Exoskeletons, 31, 41
Eye, structure of, 12–13

Fiber-optic gloves, *23*, 23–24
Field of view, 20

Force feedback, *31*, 31–32, 41
Furness, Thomas, 8

Gamemaker Namco Ltd., 17

Haptic technology, 31–32, 35
Head-mounted display (HMD), 7, *7*, *8*, 18–21, *19*
"Heads-Up" display, 8
Hearing, 6, 11, 14–16

Inner ear, 14, 26
Iowa State University, Virtual Reality Applications Center (VRAC), 43

Lens of eye, 13
Level of detail, 22

Magnetic field, 21
Magnetic sensors, 21
Mars Pathfinder mission, 41, 43
Mechanical arm, 31
Medicine, 32, 35, 36, *37*

NASA (National Aeronautics and Space Administration), 41, 43
Nausea, 14, 26
Naval Ocean Systems Center, Hawaii, 41
Naval Postgraduate School, California, 26

Perambulator, *24*
Peripheral vision, 20

PHANTOM haptic device, *31*, 35
PINCH gloves, 23
Pointing and flying, 24–26

Road-race games, 32
Rods of eye, 12

Screen display system, *28*
Shadow, 12, 18
Sight, 6, 11, 12–14
Sketchpad, 7
Smell, sense of, 6, 11
Sojourner rover, 41
Sound, 14–16, 18
Sound systems, 18, 29
Space exploration, 41, 43
Stereo glasses, *11*
Stereoscopic workbench, *10*
Super Cockpit project, *8*, *9*
Surgery, 32, 35, 36, *37*
Sutherland, Ivan, 7
Sword of Damocles, *7*, 7

Telerobotics, *38*, 39, *40*, 41
3D graphics, 20
Touch, sense of, 6, 11, 16–17
Touch devices, 18, 30–32
Tracking systems, 20–21
Treadmills, 26, *27*

2D graphics, 20

University of Chicago, Electronic Visualization Lab, 33
University of Colorado, Center for Human Simulation, *34*, 35
University of North Carolina at Chapel Hill, 26, 27, 31

Virtual reality (VR)
  beginnings of, 6–8
  fiber-optic gloves, *23*, 23–24
  in future, 41, 43–44
  haptic technology, 31–32, 35
  head-mounted display (HMD), 7, *7*, *8*, 18–21, *19*
  level of detail, 22
  many faces of, 33
  medicine, 32, 35, 36, *37*
  nausea and, 14, 26
  pointing and flying, 24–26
  reasons for, 32
  sound systems, 18, 29
  touch devices, 18, 30–32
  tracking systems, 20–21
  treadmills, 26, *27*

Wright-Patterson Air Force Base, Dayton, Ohio, 8